God Gave Us Cats To Show Us Exactly How He Sees Us

Written by
Coleman Robertson
Illustrated by
Noel Merritt

The information provided in this book is for general informational purposes only. No representations or warranties are expressed or implied about the information, products, services, or related graphics contained in this book for any purpose.

ISBN: 978-1-9990739-0-9

Cats can be both loveable and exasperating, as anyone who has been around them much can attest to. In some ways, the relationship between humans and our feline friends reflects the relationship between God and us, as per Christianity. Here are some humorous to serious observations on how cats resemble us, with biblical references.

They ignore us most of the time...
...but won't shut up when they want something from us.
Jeremiah 5:23
Psalm 5:3

When we open doors for them they're hesitant to go through...

...and often come right back in a few minutes later.

Numbers 13:26-14:4

They're nearly impossible to train.

2 Kings 17:13-14

They scare easily, scattering and hiding at the first sign of trouble.

Mark 14:27 / Matthew 26:31

They get into spats with other cats.

Isaiah 59:7
Proverbs 1:15-16

Not content with their own yard, they go and mark other cats' territory.

Job 24:2
Proverbs 22:28

They think we're reeeaaallllly impressed when they bring us dead animals.

Psalm 40:6

They leave disgusting messes for us to clean up.

Jeremiah 2:7
Isaiah 1:18

They go after forbidden food.
Genesis 3:6

Their antics are often hilarious and heartwarming.

2 Samuel 6:14

They get themselves into situations they need help to get out of.

Psalm 40:2

They hate it when we try to dunk them in water.

Luke 7:30

We get them nice things but they spurn them and go with cheap substitutes.

Exodus 32:19
Jeremiah 2:13

They often prefer to go their own way and be independent.
Isaiah 53:6

They think they're in charge of the
household.
Daniel 4:30
5:02

They can be quite affectionate when they want to be.

John 13:23

When they get lost, we are devastated...

...but when they come back to us we are overjoyed.

Luke 15:1-32

When they are sick, we go to great lengths to make them well again.

1 Peter 2:24
Romans 5:8
Mark 10:45

Despite their flaws, we love them terribly and want them to live in our house so we can dote on them and enjoy their company forever.

Psalm 52:8

www.ingramcontent.com/pod-product-compliance
Lightning Source LLC
Chambersburg PA
CBHW042145030726
47599CB00002B/622